Joy Outside the Box

written by Joy McKay

illustrated by Janaina Galhardo

Joy Outside the Box

This is a work of fiction.

Text and Illustrations copyrighted by Joy McKay ©2021

Illustrations copyrighted by A 2 Z Press LLC ©2021

Library of Congress Control Number: 2021916657

All rights reserved. No part of this book may be reproduced, transmitted, or stored in an information Retrieval system in any form or by any means, graphic, electronic, or mechanical without prior written permission from the author.

Printed in the United States of America

A 2 Z Press LLC

PO Box 582

Deleon Springs, FL 32130

bestlittleonlinebookstore.com

sizemore3630@aol.com

440-241-3126

ISBN: 978-1-954191-43-3

*To anyone that has
never fit inside a box.*

I dance everyday. I turn, I chassé and leap.

I enjoy making up dances with my dog, Tutu.

I love to dress up in my costumes.

I put on performances for my family.

I take ballet classes a few times a week from my wonderful teacher, Ms. Stephanie. I practice ballet so much my teacher encouraged me to audition for a ballet company.

She says I have what it takes to be a professional ballet dancer.

I go to the audition and before I am allowed to dance they tell me to go stand inside a box.

The box was small. I tried to dance inside the box, but my body didn't fit.

They told me that since I did not fit in the box I could not be a ballet dancer.

Why didn't I fit inside the box?

I ran so hard that I lost my balance and fell.
I fell into a ball of shame and hurt.
I started crying.

All of a sudden I heard a voice ask me a question. "Are you a ballet dancer?"

I froze. I didn't know what to say.
Could I still be a ballet dancer
even if I didn't fit inside the box?
"Are you?" I heard someone ask me again.

I stood up, wiped the tears from my eyes and said,

"Yes! I'm a ballet dancer and I don't have to fit inside a box to prove it!"

I marched. I marched all the way back up the street.

I marched back up the steps to the theater.

I marched past my mom and the dancers in the lobby.

I marched right back into the studio as someone tried to stop me.

"I don't need your box to tell me who I am and what I can do with my life! I am bigger and better than your box!"

I closed my eyes, imagining myself on stage with dancers that looked like me.

In my mind I could see the stage full of the most extraordinary dancers.

These dancers were free from the box and the ideas inside of it.

*It inspired me to dance without shame.
I felt so happy to be me.*

I was Joy outside the box.

1st Position **2nd Position**

3rd Position **4th Position** **5th Position**

"This is Joy doing a plié. Can you do a plié?"

"This is Joy doing a relevé. Can you do a relevé"

"This is Joy doing a passé. Can you do a passé?"

This is Joy doing an arabesque.
Can you do an arabesque?"

Joy McKay was born and raised in Texas. She attended the University of North Texas where she studied vocal performance. Upon moving to New York City in 2009, she attended the American Musical Dramatic Academy to pursue her passion for musical theatre. Joy is in both SAG-Aftra and AEA acting unions. She has worked professionally in TV, film, and theater.

In 2017, she created Dance With Joy NYC, focusing her dance background to teach ballet and creative movement to younger children. The program cultivates imaginative based exercises and story telling to inspire children. Joy has expanded into schools, open classes, and after school programs across Manhattan. If you are interested in her classes please check out her website <u>DanceWithJoyNYC.com</u>.

Don't just dance for fun, Dance With Joy!

CPSIA information can be obtained
at www.ICGtesting.com
Printed in the USA
BVHW091321220222
629774BV00019B/1465